Sandhya &

#78
Vishwa Mitra Arya Samaj Mandir

Edit & Published by

Suknanand Bharat (Rickey)

And Family

(Venita, Nityanand, Chidanand Bharat)

rickeybharat@gmail.com

SANDHYA

Maharshi Dayanand Saraswati has defined Sandhya as the meditation
in which one concentrates on GOD. It should be done at the time when day and night meet each other i.e. early in the morning at sun-rise or dawn and in the evening at sun-set or dusk.

"Purvaa Sandhyam Japamsitishthet
Sawitrimaarkadarshanat,
Pashchimam Tu Samaaseenah Samyagriksha
Vimaavanaat".
(Manu.2-101)
means: " At the morning twilight let him stand muttering the "Savitri" till he has seen the sun; at the evening , (let him) seated (mutter it), till constellations clearly appear." (Manu. 2-101)

"Standing and muttering (the Gayatri Mantra) at the morning twilight, he removes nocturnal sin; but seated at the evening twilight, he destroys sin done by day." (Manu 2.102)

Sandhya is the personal relationship with GOD because only He is the one who is the "Nearest and Dearest".

ATHA SANDHYO-PAASA-NAA VIDHIH

MANTRA 1

AA-CHAM-ANA

Sipping sacramental water as amrita, the nectar of
deathlessness, and asking for a life filled with happiness.
Chant the mantra once and sip water thrice.

**Om shanno deveer abisthtaya
aapo bhavantu peetaye
shanyor abhi-sravantu nah.** *Yajur Veda 36:12*

Devee swaroop eeshwar pooran abheesht keeje
Yah neer ho sudhaa-mai kalyaan daan deeje
Nit riddhi siddhi barse hit ho sadaa hamaraa
Behtee rahe hridai me sad-dharm prem dhaara

TRANSLATION

O All-pervading Mother, Sweet and Divine,
Be pleased to bless the cravings of my soul
To reach thy bosom. May this world of mine
Be filled with peace and bliss from pole to pole.

MANTRA 2

INDRIYA SPARSHA

Touching the limbs with water, and praying that these limbs may earn me fame (yasha) and strength (bala).

Om vaak vaak ... (Touch lips)
Om praanah praanah ...(nostrils)
Om chakshuh chakshuh ... (eyes)
Om shrotram shrotram ... (ears)
Om naabhih ...(navel)
Om hridayam ... (heart)
Om kanthah ... (throat)
Om shirah ...(head)
Om baahu-bhyaam yasho-balam ...(shoulders)
Om kara-tala kara-prishthe ... (palms and their sides)

Tan man vachan se honge, ham shuddh karm kaaree
Dus-karm se bachengee, sab indriyaa hamaaree
Vaanee vishuddh hogee, priya praan punya-shaalee
Hongee hamaaree aakhe, ye divya jyoti-waalee
Ye kaan jyaan bhooshit, ye naabhi pushti-kaaree
Hogaa hridai, Dayaamai! samyak sudharm dhaaree
Bhagawaan! teree gaathaa, gaayegaa kanth meraa
Sir me sadaa ramegaa, gaurav gurutwa teraa
Honge ye haath mere yash oj tej-dharee
Meree hathe-liyaa bhee hongee pavitra pyaare

TRANSLATION

I make a vow before Thy sacred Throne
To try and hold my mortal heart away
From sin; my human ograns shall be prone
To keep the world I give Thee on this day.
My tongue, my nose and both the sides of palm,
My eyes, my ears, the genitals and my heart
My hands, my throat, and head, serene and calm,
Will sure remain from sinful deeds apart.

MANTRA 3

MAARJANA:

Touching the limbs again with water, and invoking God's
help in cleansing them of impurity.

Om bhooh punaatu shirasi ... (Forehead)
Om bhuwah punaatu netrayoh ... (Eyes)
Om swah punaatu kanthe ... (Throat)
Om maha punaatu hridaye ... (Heart)
Om janah punaatu naabhyaam ... (Navel)
Om tapah punaatu punah paadayoh ...
(Feet)
Om satyam punaatu punah shirasi
...(Head)
Om khambrahma punaatu sarvatra ...(All
over)

Jeewan swaroop jag-pati! mastak pavitra kardo
Dayaar-dra ho dayaamai! nai-no me jyoti bhardo
Aanand roop adheesh-war! hamko sukanth deejee
Bhagawan! hridai sadam me, hardam niwaas keeje
Jag ke janak hamaaree ho naabhi nir-vikaaree
Pad bhee pavitra howe, he sarv jyaan dhaaree
Puni puni puneet sir ho, he satya roop swaamee
sarvaang shuddh owe, vyaapak vibho namaamee

TRANSLATION.

But Glorious Father! I am weak and frail
And hence depend on Thy Loving Grace,
My sole efforts will not, O Lord , avail
The frightful host of heinous sins to face.
So, therefore, Lord, I meekly pray to Thee
To make me pure in mind, and too strong
To yield to tempting sins. O make me free
To sit in peace and sing Thy Glory's song.
O Living, Holy, Happy Father, Great,
The Wise and Omnipresent King of all,
The Sole Eternal Master of my fate,
My mind and soul Thy gracious blessings call
To make my head, my eyes and passions pure,
To change my vicious heart; and guide my feet,
To grace my brain and throat, and make it sure
That sin will nowhere find a welcome seat.

MANTRA 4

PRAANAA-YAAMA:

Controlling the breath and contemplating the qualities of
the Supreme Lord.

(Forcefully exhale, and keep the breath out for as long as
you can. Then, inhale gently, slowly, and deeply, while
mentally chanting the following mantra. This is one
Praanayam. Perform three Pranaayaam.)

Om bhooh
Om bhuwah
Om swah
Om mahah
Om janah
Om tapah
Om satyam

TRANSLATION

The Supreme Lord is: Bhooh - Dearer than breath, and
Basis of all existence.
Bhuwah- Dispeller of all pains, Origin of all becoming
Swah - Bestower of happiness
Mahah - Worthy of worship, and the Fount of greatness
Janah - Origin of creativity
Tapah - Impeller of action
Satyam - Personification of Truth

I hold my breath in sacred awe and pray
O God of Life, O Holy God of Bliss;
O Father, Great and Wise, and True, this day
My soul arrives Thy Glorious Feet to kiss.

MANTRA 5

AGHA-MARSHANA

Discovering the process of the creation of the universe,
and identifying God as the Creator, Sustainer and
Destroyer, in an effort to decrease the tendency to commit
sin.

**Om Ritancha sat-yanchaa bheed
dhaat-tapaso 'dhya-jaayata.
Tato raatr-ya-jaayata
tatah samudro arnavah**

TRANSLATION

By God's command His Nature brought to light
The principles and the atoms of this earth.
Then came chaos and heat and motion bright,
And then the waves of ocean got their birth.

MANTRA 6

Samudraad arnavaad adhi samvatsaro ajaa-yata. Aho-raa-traani vida-dhad vishwasya mishato vashee

TRANSLATION

And after these the planets moved aright
Along the annual course of heaven blue.
The King of all creates the day and night,
Without effort and their order due.

MANTRA 7

Sooryaa chandra-masau dhaataa yathaa poorvam akal-payat Divam cha prithiveem chaanta-rik-sham atho swah.

TRANSLATION

And, as before, the Maker made again
The sun, the moon, and bodies dark and bright,
The sky above, the place unknown to pain -
The home of bliss – the Realm of Holy Light.

MANASAA PARI-KRAMAA:

Certifying the Presence of God in all directions, and expressing gratitude for the bounties He provides for achieving perfection.

MANTRA 8

Om Praachee dig-agnir adhi-patir
asito rakshitaa dityaa ishavah.
Tebhyo namo 'dhipati-bhyo
namo rakshi-tribhyo
nama ishu-bhyo nama ebhyo astu.
Yo's maan dweshti yam vayam dwishmas
tam wo jambhe dadhmah.

TRANSLATION

Thou art before us, Father Good and Wise!
The Mighty King Who saves the world from woes
Who made the sun that from the East does rise
And on this earth its beams of luster throws-
The lustrous beams which shower life on earth
And make us living through Thy blessed grace.
O Lord, to thank Thee for Thy gift of life
We bend our knees before Thy Holy Face.
We also thank thee for thy rule benign
Thy kind protection and Thy blessings sweet
And those who are the dreaded foes of mine
I lay them humbly at Thy Gracious Feet.

MANTRA 9

Dakshinaa dig indro 'dhi-patis
tirash-chi-raajee rakshitaa pitara ishavah.
Tebhyo namo 'dhipati-bhyo
namo rakshi-tribhyo
nama ishu-bhyo nama ebhyo astu.
Yo's maan dweshti
yam vayam dwishmas
tam wo jambhe dadhmah.

O Mighty Sovereign! Thou art to our right
The Great protector from the dreaded brood
Of boneless reptiles. Lord of Vedic Light!
Thy sages come to teach us what is good.
We also thank Thee for Thy rule benign
Thy kind protection and Thy blessings sweet
And those who are the dreaded foes of mine
I lay them humbly at Thy Gracious Feet.

MANTRA 10

Prateechee dig varuno 'dhi-patih
pri-daa-koo rakshitaan-na mishavah.
Tebhyo namo 'dhipati-bhyo
namo rakshi-tribhyo
nama ishu-bhyo nama ebhyo astu.
Yo's maan dweshti yam vayam dwishmas
tam wo jambhe dadhmah.

TRANSLATION

Thou are behind us, gracious King, adored,
As Great Protector from bony beasts
Thou savest our humble lives having stored
The hungry earth, O Lord, with human feast.
We also thank thee for thy rule benign
Thy kind protection and thy blessings sweet
And those who are the dreaded foes of mine
I lay them humbly at Thy Gracious Feet.

MANTRA 11

Udeechee dik somo 'dhi-patih
swajo rakshitaa shanir ishavah.
Tebhyo namo 'dhipati-bhyo
namo rakshi-tribhyo
nama ishu-bhyo nama ebhyo astu.
Yo's maan dweshti yam vayam dwishmas
tam wo jambhe dadhmah.

TRANSLATION

Thou art to our left, O Peaceful King
To save us from the self-borne insects' bane
By Nature's heat. Thy praise we humbly sing,
O Loving Savior from the pangs of pain!
We also thank thee for thy rule benign
Thy kind protection and thy blessings sweet
And those who are the dreaded foes of mine
I lay them humbly at Thy Gracious Feet.

MANTRA 12

Dhruvaa dig Vishnu radhi-pathih
kal-maasha-greevo raakshitaa vee-ru-dha
ishavah.
Tebhyo namo 'dhipati-bhyo
namo rakshi-tribhyo
nama ishu-bhyo nama ebhyo astu.
Yo's maan dweshti yam vayam dwishmas
tam wo jambhe dadhmah.

TRANSLATION

Thou art below us, Omnipresent King
To nourish life with plants of tuberous roots
And verdant trees that leafy shelter bring,
And yield to us ten thousand kinds of fruits.
We also thank Thee for Thy rule benign
Thy kind protection and Thy blessings sweet
And those who are the dreaded foes of mine
I lay them humbly at Thy Gracious Feet.

MANTRA 13

Oor-dhwaa dig brihas-patir adhi-patih
shwi-tro rakshitaa varsha mishavah
Tebhyo namo 'dhipati-bhyonamo rakshi-
tribhyo
nama ishu-bhyo nama ebhyo astu
Yo's maan dweshti
yam vayam dwishmas
tam wo jambhe dadhmah.

TRANSLATION
Thou art above us, Great and Holy King
To develop and protect us on this earth.
Thy grace the vital drops of rain doth bring
To fill with corn the seat of mortal birth.
We also thank thee for thy rule benign
Thy kind protection and thy blessings sweet
And those who are the dreaded foes of mine
I lay them humbly at Thy Gracious Feet.

UPA-STHAANA

Feeling the living presence of God after having a direct
vision of Him.(**Mantras 14- 17**)

**Om Ud-vayam tama-sas pari
swah pashyanta ut-taram.
Devam devatraa sooryam
aganma jyotir ut-tamam.**

TRANSLATION

May I obtain the glorious God of Light
The wisest God of Bliss and Lord Supreme
The Sun that keeps the souls of mortals bright
And forms my humble prayer's sacred theme.

MANTRA 15

**Udut-yam jaatavedasam
devam vahanti ketavah.
Drishe vish-waaya sooryam.**

TRANSLATION

The various objects of this wondrous earth
Are beacon flags to guide us on to know
The Glorious Sun of Life Who gave us birth
And sent his Veda the righteous path to show.

MANTRA 16

Chitram devaanaam ud-agaad aneekam
chakshur mitrasya varunasya-agneh.
Aapraa dyaawaa pri-thi-vee antariksham
soorya aatamaa jagatas tas-thu-shash cha,
swaahaa!

TRANSLATION

How wondrous is this Lord of Holy Light
The sun's support, the God of moon, the Source
Of shining bodies, the Lord of fire bright
The heaven's Lord, the King of earth, the Force
That made the sky and countless kinds of things
That move and do not move. O Lord of might,
My humble heart Thy sacred prayer sings
To let me think, speak and act aright.

MANTRA 17

Tach chakshur devahitam
purastaach chhukram uch-charat.
Pashyema sharadah shatam
Jeevema sharadah shatan
Shrinu-yaama sharadah shatam
Pra-bra-vaama sharadah shatam
Adeenaah syaama sharadah shatam
Bhooyash cha sharadah shataat.

TRANSLATION

That Ever-wakeful Eye, Eternal, Pure
That watches close the deeds of right and wrong
Whose Holy Grace the learned souls secure
May bless in life my prayer's sacred song.
And may we live and see a hundred years,
A hundred autumns hear His Holy Name,
And sing His Glory free from human fears

That close attend the heels of earthly fame.
And if we live for more than a hundred years,
The same delight attend us all the days
We live, and bring us all the sacred cheers
For which the heart to gracious heaven prays.

MANTRA 18

ATHA BRAHMA GAAYATREE SAAVITREE GURU MANTRA:

Chanting the Gaayatree Mantra, which is the sacred-most of all Vedic Mantras, and which has been taught in a disciple succession, so that we can discover a source of inspiration.

Om bhoor bhuwah swah.
Tat savitur varenyam
bhargo devasya dheemahi.
Dhiyo nah pracho-dayaat.

God is Dear to me like my own breath. He is the Dispeller of my pains, and the Giver of happiness. I meditate on the supremely adorable Light of the Divine Creator, that It may inspire my thought and understanding.

O Soul of Life, the Holy King of kings!
O God of all the regions, high and low,
O Lord of Joy, Whose Glory Nature sings,
Who shapes the earth and lets the mortals grow.
We seek Thy blessed Feet to meditate
Upon Thy Glorious Form of Holy Light
Which drives away the gloom of sins we hate
And makes the souls of righteous people bright.

My heart, O Father, meekly prays to Thee
To win Thy Grace, to make me good and wise,
And bless my mind with knowledge, full and free
From dark and vicious thoughts of sins and lies.

MANTRA 19

SAMARPANA
Surrender and Dedication

**He eesh-wara dayaa-nidhe!
Bhawat kripa-yaa 'nena
Japo-paa-sanaa-di karmanaa
Dhar-maartha kaama mok-shaa-naam
Sadyah siddhir bhawen-nah**

TRANSLATION

O Lord! O Infinite Treasure of Mercy! By Your Grace, may we very soon realize Dharma (righteous living), Arthaa (righteous wealth), Kaama (righteous enjoyment), and Moksha (emancipation from the world) through our Japa (recitation of God's Name) and Upaasanaa (communion with God.

MANTRA 20

NAMASKAARA:

Tata Eeshwaram Namas-kuryaat
Final Obeisance

**Om namah sham-bhawaaya cha
mayo bhawaaya cha
namah shanka-raaya cha
mayas-karaaya cha
namah shivaaya cha
shiva taraaya cha.**

He mangalesh shankar! mangal karo hamaaraa
Paawan prakash paa-e, para-maarth punya dwaaraa
Parijyaan paya pilaado, awa-dhar a-gaadh daanee
Teree sharan me aayaa, hai bhakta yah 'Bhawaanee'

Ham baar baar bhagavan! karte tumhe namaste
Yadi dwesh bhaa-wa-naa ho, to nyaaya tere haste

TRANSLATION
And now I bow to Thee, O God of calm,
O God of Peace, and Lord of Bliss Divine!
Thy Grace supplies to burning hearts a balm,
Thy blessings in my right desires shine!

We also thank thee for thy rule benign
Thy kind protection and Thy blessings sweet
And those who are the dreaded foes of mine
I lay them humbly at Thy Gracious Feet.

Om Shaantih - Cosmic peace!
Shaantih - Spritual peace!!
Shaantih - Material peace!!!

Iti Sandhyo-paasa-naa vidhih

~Here comes to an end the Sandhyaa Meditation~

 # HAVAN

Havan is an age-old sacred rituals to propitiate various deities using the sacred fire as a medium for the attainment of various wishes and boons in the materialistic and the spiritual worlds.

We do Havan to dispel the negative energies from our minds; to destroy negative life patterns; to annihilate negative effects and evils of others.

Havan also brings high energies into our minds and body thereby paving

In short Havan does the following:

Invokes blessings and grace of God in our lives
Awakens our auspicious energies.
Cleanses our body and mind and Clenses the atmosphere

<u>ATHAA-CHA-MANAM</u>

Aachamana is the sipping of sacrificial water from the right palm.
This is the first act before the performance of the Agnihotra Sacrifice. The aspirant seeks to symbolically wash his self of all impurity.

Om amrito pas-taranam-asi swaahaa.
O divine waters of knowledge! You are the spread of eternal life.

Om amrita-pidhaanam-asi swaahaa.
O divine water of knowledge! You are the covering of eternal life

Om satyam yashah shreer mayi shreeh shra-ya-taam swaahaa.
May wealth, consisting of truth, fame and riches take refuge in me

ATHAANGA SPARSHA

As we touch the body limbs with sacrificial water, we pray that these remain strong and fulfil their fuctions.

Om vaang ma aasye 'stu (lips)

Om nasor me praano 'stu (nostrils)

Om akshnor me chakshur astu (eyes)

Om karna-yor me shro-tram astu. (ears)

Om baah-wor me balam astu. (arms)

Om oor-wor ma ojo 'stu. (thighs)

Om arish-taani me 'ngaani tanoos
Tanwaa me saha santu (all over)

May the speech in my mouth be sanctified in God.
May the breath in my nostrils, the sight in my eyes, and the hearing in my ears be sanctified in god.
May the force in my arms and legs be sanctified in god.
May my limbs be all unharmed. And may my outer self be harmony with my inner self.

ATESHWARA STUTI PRAAR-THANO-PAASANAAH

Here we begin the Eeshwar Stuti, Praarthanaa,
Upaasana the Glorification of, Prayer to, and
Communion with God.

Om vishwaani deva savitar duritaani paraa-
suva.
Yad bhadram tan-na aasuva.

Om hiranya-garbhah sama-var-tataa-gre
Bhootasya jaatah patir eka aaseet.
Sa daa-dhaara prithiveem dyaam utemaam
Kasmai devaaya havishaa vidhema

Om ya aat-madaa bala-daa yasya vishwa
upaasate prashisham yasya devaah.
Yasya chhaayaa'mritam yasya mrityuh
kasmai devaaya havishaa vidhema

Om yah praana-to nimisha-to mahit-waika
Id raajaa jagato babhoowa.
Ya eeshe asya dwipa-dash chatush-padah
Kasmai devaaya havishaa vidhema

Om yena dyaur-ugraa prithivee cha dridhaa
Yena swah stabhitam yena naakah.
Yo antarikshe rajaso vimaanah
Kasmai devaaya havishaa vidhema

Om prajaa-pate! Na twad etaan-yanyo
Vishwaa jaataani pari taa babhoowa.
Yat kaamaas-te juhumas tan-no astu
Vayam syaama patayo rayeenaam.

Om san no bandhur janitaa sa vidhaataa
Dhaamaani veda bhuwa-naani vishwaa.
Yatra devaa amritam aa-na-shaanaas
Triteeye dhaaman na-dhyair-ayanta.

Om agne! Naya su-pathaa raaye asmaan
Vishwaani deva vayunaani vidwaan.
Yuyo-dhyas-maj juhuraanam eno
Bhooyish-thaan te nama uktim vidhema.

He sakal jagat ke utpatti karta,samagra
eshvarya ukta, sud-svaroop, sarv sukho ke
daataa parmeshvar aap kripaa karke hamaare
sampurn durgundurvyasan aur dukho ko dur
kejiye. Jo kaliyarn kaarak gun karm svabhaa
waale padarat hai, way sab hamko praapt
karaa-eyea.

O Lord, progenitor, creator of the universe,
source of all happiness, we pray thee to wipe
off all our vices, evil desires and distress and
place upon good deeds, create the desire for
the good ways and the righteous nature and
give us moral strength that may bring bliss to
us.

ATHA SVASTI – VAACHANAM
Prayer for Bliss and Prosperity

OM agnim-eelee purohitam yajnasya
devaam-ritvi-jam, hootaaram ratna
dhaatamam.

Om sa nah piteva ssonave'gne soopaayano
bhava. Sachas-waa nah svastaye.

Om swasti no mimetaam-ashwinaa bhagah
Swasti dev-yaditir anar-vanah.
Swasti pooshaa asuro dadhaatu nah
Swasti dyaawaa prithivee suche-tunaa.

Om swastaye vaayu-mupa bravaa-mahai
Somam swasti bhuwa-nasya yas patih
Brihaspatim savaganam swastaye
Swastaya aadit-yaaso bhawantu nah.

Om vishwe devaa no adya swastaye
Vaish-waa-naro vasu-ragnih swastaye.
Devaa avantu ribhawah swastaye
Swasti no rudrah paat-wang-hasah.

Om swasti mitraa varunaa
Swasti pathye revati
Swasti na indrash chaag-nish cha
Swasti no adite kridhi.

Om swasti panthaam anucharema
Sooryaa Chandra-masaa viva.
Punar dada-taagh-nataa
Jaanaa-taa sanga-memahi.

Hay gyaan svaroop parmeshvar, gaise putra kaleya,
Pita gyaan data hota hai, waise aap hamaare lyea, such kay hay too, pradark took-tkee prapti, karanay walay hoyay.

O Lord the source of all knowledge we pray thee
To enlighten us with true knowledge, so that we may
have ready access to thee as a son has to his father.
May we co-operate with one another and remain
united for the attainment of bliss and true happiness

Anger Destroys The Beauty Of The Heart As Well As
The Beauty Of The Face

In Silence We Find A Solution To Every Problem

Respect Is Received When It Is Given

ATHA SHAANTI – PRAKARANAM
Prayer For Peace And Harmony

Om shanna indraagni bhawataam avobhih
Shanna indraa varunaa raata-havyaa.
Shamindraa soma su-vi-taaya shamyoh
Shanna indraa poosha-naa vaaja-saatau

Om shanno bhagah shamu nah shanso
astu. Shannah puran-dhih shamu santu
raayah. Shannah satyasya su-yamasya
shansah. Shanno aryamaa puru-jaato astu

Om shanno dhaataa shamu dhartaa no
astu. Shanna u-roo-chee bhawatu swa-
dhaabhih Sham rodasee brihatee shanno
adrih. Shanno dewaanaam suha-waani
santu.

Om shanno agnir jyotir aneeko astu
Shanno mitraa varunaa vash-vinaa sham.
Shannah sukritaam sukri-taani santu.
Shanna ishiro abhi-vaatu vaatah.

Om shanno dyaava prithivee poorva-
hootau. Sham anta-riksham drishaye no
astu.
Shanna osha-dheer vanino bhawantu
Shanno rajas as patir-astu jishnuh.

Om shanna indro vasu-bir devo astu
Sham aaditye-bhir varunah su-shansah.
Shanno rudro rudre-bhir jalaashah
Shannas twash-taag-naa-bhi-riha shrinotu.

Om shannah somo bhavatu brahma shannah. Shanno graa-vaanah shamu santu yaj-yaah. Shannah swaroo-naam mitayo bhawantu
Shannah praswah sham vastu vedih.

Bhagavaan! Hamaaree eashvarya shanti-daayak ho,
Hamaaree prasanasaa shanti-daayak ho
Hamaaree buddhi shanti dayak ho, Sab
prakaar ka dhan shanti dayak ho, Shasshan
shanti dayak ho, shesto ka maan
Karne waalaa nyaya-kaaree bhagvan shanti
dayak ho.

May the vegetable kingdom bring us peace and harmony. May the all round knowledge of the material world bring happiness to us. May we derive the fullest benefit from mother earth. May our experiments be blessed with successes and may the pillars of our buildings be built on good foundation and may our houses be well designed. May the stores of grain and children in the household bring us peace and happiness.

ATHA SHIVA SANKALPA MANTRAAH

Om yaj jaagrato dooram udaiti daivam,
Tadu suptasya tathai-vaithi,
Doo-ranga-mam jyotishaam jyoti-rekam,
Tan-me manah shiva-sankalpam astu.
*(may that my mind be filled with beautiful and
benevolent thoughts)*
Om yena karmaan-yapaso manee-shino
Yaj-ye krinvanti vida-the-shu dheerah.
Yada-poorvam yak-sham antah prajaa-
naam,
Tan-me manah shiva-sankalpam astu

Om yat praj-yaanam uta cheto
Dhritish cha yaj-jyotir antar
Amritam prajaasu. Yasmaan na rite
Kin-chana karma kriyate
Tan-me manah shiva-sankalpam astu.

Om yene-dam bhootam bhuwa-nam
Bhavish-yat pari-gri-heetam
Amritena sarvam.yena yaj-yas
Taayate sapta hotaa,
Tan-me manah shiva-sankalpam astu.

Om yasminn richah saama yajoomshi
yasmin Pratish-thi-taa ratha-naa-bhaa-vi-
vaa-raah. Yas-minsh-chittam sarva-motam
prajaa-naam
Tan-me manah shiva-sankalpam astu.

Om su-shaa-rathir ash-waan iva yan
manushyaan
Ne-nee-yate bhee-shu-bhir vaa-jina iva.
Hrit pra-tish-tham yada-jiram javish-tham
Tan-me manah shiva-sankalpam astu

Om sa nah pawas-wa shanga-ve
Sham janaaya sha-mar-vate.
Sham raajan-nosha-dhee-bhyah.
*Bring peace to the world of animals with your flow, o
king and peace to the world of human beings,too.
Peace, indeed, to the world of trees and plants*

Om abhayam mitraad abhayama mitraad
Abhayam jyaa-taad abhayam parok-shaat.
Abhayam naktam abhayam diva nah
Sarvaa aashaa mama mitram bhawantu.

*No fear from the friend,nor from the enemy, No fear
from the known, nor from the unknown . No fear in
the night, nor in the day.
May we be friends unto all directions, and may all
directions be friendly unto us*

Iti Shaanti Parkaranam
*Here comes to an end of the Shaanti Prakaranam
chant*

ॐ

ATHA-AGNI-HOTRAM
Here begins the Agnihotra Sacrifice

AGNI PRA-DEE-PANA
Kindling the sacrificial fire

1. Om bhoor bhuwah swah.

AGNI AADHAANA
Placing the sacrificial fire in the Kunda.

2. Om bhoor bhuwah swar dyau-riva
bhoomnaa
Prithi-veeva varimnaa. Tasyaas-te prithivi
deva-yajani!
Prish-the'gni manna da-mannaa dyaayaa
dadhe.

AGNI SAMINDHANA
Fanning the fire

3. Om ud-budhyas-waagne prati-jaagrihi
Twam ishtaa poorte sam-srije-thaam
Ayan cha. Asmint sa-dhaste adhyut-
tarasmin
Vishwe dewaa yaja-maanash cha seedata

SAMIDAADHAANA

Oblations with three sacrificial pieces of wood.

4. Om ayanta idhma aatmaa jaata-vedas
Tene-dhyaswa var-dhaswa ched-dha
Vardhaya chaas-maan praja-yaa
Pashu-bhir brahma-varchase
Naan-naa-dyena samedhaya swaahaa.
Idam agnaye jaataa-vedase, idanna mama (*offer
first samidhaa*)

5. Om samidhaagnim duwasyata ghritair
Bodhaya taa-ti-thim. Aasmin havyaa
Juho-tana
Om susamid-dhaaya sho-chi-she gritam
Teevram juhotana. Agnaye
Jaata-vedase swaahaa.
Idam agnaye jaata-vedase, idanna mama.
(*offer the second samidhaa*)

6. Om tantwaa samid-bhirangiro ghritena
Vardha-yaamasi. Brihach chho-chaa
Ya-vish-thya swaahaa.
Idam agnaye angirase, idanna mama. (*Offer
the third samidha*)

PANCHA GHRIT AAHUTI
Five ghee oblations
Symbolise the five daily duty of a person

7. Om ayanta idhma aatmaa jaata-vedas
tene-dhyaswa
Var-dhaswa ched-dha vardhaya chaas-
maan praja-yaa
Pashu-bhir brahma-varchase naan-naa-
dyena Samedhaya swaahaa.
Idam agnaye jaataa-vedase, idanna mama

JALA SINCHANA
Fill the right palm with water and
Around the kunda as directed

8. Om adite 'nu-man-yaswa.   *(East)*
9. Om animate 'nu-man-yaswa.   *(West)*
10. Om saraswat-yanu-man-yaswa *(North)*
11. Om deva savitah prasuva yajyam
Prasuva jajya-patim bhagaaya. Divyo
gandharwah keta-pooh ketan-nah punaatu
vaachas-patir vaachan-nah swa-da-tu.
(sprinkle all around the kund clockwise from
east to east)

AAGHAA-RAAV-AAJYA BHAAG AAHUTI
Four ghee oblations

12. Om agnaye swaahaa.
Idam agnaye, idanna mama.
(make oblations onto the fire, to the north)

13. Om somaaya swaahaa.
Idam somaaya, idanna mama
(make oblation onto the fire, to the South)

14. Om prajaa-pataye swaahaa
Idam prajaa-pataye, idanna mama
(make oblation onto the fire, to the center)

15. Om indraaya swaahaa.
Idam indraaya, idanna mama
(center)

VYAAHRITI AAHUTI
Ghee oblation con't
16. Om Bhoor agnaye swaahaa.
Idam agnaye,idanna mama

17. Om Bhuwar vaayave swaahaa
Idam vaayave, idanna mama

18. Om Swar aadityaaya swaahaa.
Idam aadityaaya, idanna mama

19. Om Bhoor bhuwah swaragni vaayvaa-
Dityebhyah swaahaa
Idam agni vaayvaa-dityebhyah, idanna
mama

BRIHAD VISHESH YAJNA
Mantras Oblations for Special Occasions
PAVA-MAAN AAHUTI
Oblation for Purification and Enlightenment

Om ....swaahaa. Idam
prajaapataye idanna mama.*(silently)*

20. Om bhoor-bhuwaha swah. Agna
aayoomshi pawasa aa-suvor jamisham cha
nah. Aare baadhas-wa duch-chhu-naam
swaahaa.
Idam agnaye pawa-maanaa-ya, idanna
mama.

21. Om bhoor bhuwah swah. Agnir rishih
pawa-maanah paancha-janyah purohitah.
Tamee-mahe mahaan-gayam swaahaa.
Idam agnaye pawa-maanaaye-ya, idanna
mama

22. Om bhoor bhuwah swah. Agne pawas-
wa swa-paa asme varchah su-veeryam.
Dadhad rayim mahi posham swaahaa.
Idam agnaye pawa-maanaa-ya, idanna
mama

23. Om bhoor bhuwah swah. Prajaa-pate
na twad etaan-yanyo vishwaa jaataani pari
taa babhoowa. Yat kaamaas-te juhumas
tan-no astu vayam syaama patayo
rayeenaam swaahaa.
Idam prajaa-pataye, idanna mama

PRATAH KAAL AAHUTI
Morning Ghee-Saamagree Oblations

24. Om sooryo jyotir jyotih sooryah
swaahaa

25. Om sooryo varcho jyotir varchah
swaahaa

26. Om jyotih sooryah sooryo jyotih
swaahaa.

27. Om sajoor devena savitraa sajoo-
rusha-sendra-vatyaa.
Jushaanah sooryo vetu swaahaa

SAAYAM – KAALA AAHUTI
Evening Ghee-saamagree oblation

28. Om agnir jyotir jyotir agnih swaahaa.

29. Om agnir varcho jyotir varchah
swaahaa.

30. Om agnir jyotir jyotir agnih swaahaa
(silently)

31. Om sajoor devena savitraa sajoo-
ratryen-dra-Vatyaa. Jushaano agnir vetu
swaahaa.

PRAATAH SAAYAM AAHUTI

Morning Evening Oblations Of Ghee and Saamagree.

32. Om bhoo-rag-naye praanaya swaahaa.
Idam agnaye praanaaya, idanna mama.

33. Om bhuwar-waaya-ve' paanaaya
swaahaa.
Idam waaya-ve' paanaaya,idanna mama

34. Om swar-aadit-yaaya vyaanaa-ya
swaahaa.
Idam aadityaaya vyaanaaya,idanna mama

35. Om bhoor bhuwah swaragni vaay-
vaaditye Bhyah praanaa-paana vyaane-
bhyah swaahaa. Idam agni vaay-vaa-ditye-
bhyah Praanaa-paana vyaane-
bhyah,idanna mama.

36. Om aapo jyootee raso'mritam brahma
Bhoor bhuwah swar-om swaahaa.

37. Om yam medhaam deva-ganaah
pitarash Cho-paa-sate. Tayaa maa-madya
Medhayaag-ne Medhaa-vinam kuru
swaahaa.

38. Om vishwaani deva savitar duritaani
Paraa-suva. Yad bhadram tan-na aasuva
swaahaa.

Take away from my mind, Radiant creator,all tendencies To transgress your laws, bringing unto me, instead, all that is beautiful Benevolent and auspious.

39. Om agne naya su-pathaa raaye asmaan Vishwaani deva vayu-naani vidwaan. Yuyo-dyas-maj juhuraanam eno bhooyish Than te nama uktim vidhema swaahaa.

ATHA BRAHMA GAAYATREE SAAVITREE GURU MANTRA

40. Om bhoor bhuwah swah. Tat savitur varenyam Bhargo devasya dheemahi. Dhiyo yo nah Pracho-dayaat swaahaa.

He dayaalu parmaatman! Aap apne aaseem kripaa se hamare
Sadaa rakshaa karte hai. Aap hee hamaare jeevan-aadhaar hai.
Apne sevako ke dukho ko door karke unko sukh dene-waale hai.
Aap sarvatra supra-tish-tit aur suprasidha hai.
Aap sarva-uttam,shuddha,pavitra aur gyaan swaroop hai. Aap se hee yah saaraa jagat utt-pan huaa hai. Aap hee sakal shubha gunno ko khan hai. Aap kaa ham prati-din dhyaan kare aur aap Hame vivek-sheeltaa dhaar-naa-vati medhaa sad-buddhi pradaan kare.

O supreme Lord, the source of Existence,
Intelligence and bliss,
Creator of the Universe,
May we prove worthy of thee,
May we meet thy glorious grace,
May us thou be the unerring guide of our minds,
And may we follow thy lead unto righteousness.

O soul of life the holy king of kings
O God of all the regions high and low
O lord of joy, whose glory nature sings,
Who shapes the earth and let the mortal
grow.

We seek thy blessed feet to meditate,
Upon thy glorious form of holy light,
Which drive away the gloom of sins we hate
And make the soul of righteousness people
bright.

Our heart, O father, meekly prays to thee
To win thy grace to make us good and wise,
And bless the mind with knowledge full and
free From dark and vicious thoughts of sins
and lies

SWISHTA-KRIT-AAHUTI
Oblation for Atonement

40. Om yad asya karmano'tyaree-richam
Yad waa nyoonam ihaa karam. Agnish tat
Swishta-krid vidyaat sarvam swish-tam Su-
hutam karoyu me. Agnaye swishta-krite su-
huta-hute sarva-praayash-chittaa-hutee-
naam
kaamaa-naam samara-dhayi-tre sarvaan
nah kaamaant samardhaya swaahaa.
Idam agnaye swishta krite, idanna mama

Whatever in our performance we have done superfluous, Whatever we have done that ought not to be done, May the radiant one, the fulfiller, full fill it all, harmonise it With our intent and make it all well-performed and well-offered.

We beseech him who is the full filler of all wishes, who Accepts all confession and repentance, and who grant the realisation of all that be willed, grant thou unto us the fulfilment of all our wishes, O lord, this is truly done unto the radiant one the fulfiller, it is no more ours.

41. Om namah sham bhavaya cha, mayo bhavaya cha, Namah shankaraya cha, mayaskaraya cha
Namah shivaya cha, shivatarya cha.
Swaahaa

42.   Om purnamadha purnam idam purnaat-purnmud-chyatay Purnasya purnmaadaaya purn-mayvaa-v ashesh-yatay, swaahaa

43. Om sarvam vai poorna gvam swaahaa (3 Times)

ALL IS PERFECT ALL IS COMPLETE

44   Om vasoh pavitramase satdhaaram, vasoh pavitra mase Shastra-daaram. Devastvaa savitaa poonatu vasoh Pavitrain satdhaarain supava kaam duksha.

ATHA MUKHA SPARSHAH
*With out-stretched palms facing the holy
fire pass lightly over face*

Om tanoopaa agne'si
Tanwam me paahi.

Om aayur-daa agne 'si
aayur me dehi.

Om varcho-daa agne'se
Varcho me dehi.

Om agne yan –me tanwaa
Oonam tan-ma aa-prina.

Om medhaam me devah
Savitaa aa-da-dhaatu

Om medhaam me devee
Saraswatee aa-da-dhaatu

Om medhaam me ashvi-nau
Devaa-vaa dhattaam
Push-karas-rajau.

46.   ATHA ANGA SPARSHAH
With both palms, touch the body-limbs.

Om vaak cha ma aa- pyaa yataam
(lip)
Om praa-nash cha ma aa-pyaa yataam
(nose)
Om chak-shush cha ma aa-pyaa
yataam   (eyes)
Om shrotram cha ma aa-pyaa-yataam
(ears)
Om yasho-balam cha ma aa-pyaa-
yataam   (shoulders)

Let my speech find fulfilment. Let my
breathing, seeing and
hearing be fulfilled. Let my arms earn me
fame and strength

Om stuta mayaa varda veda-mata, pracho dayantaam Powamanie duj jaanaam. Aayuh praanaam prajaam pashum Keertim dravinaam brahma varchasaam mahiyam daltvaa varjataa Brahma ha – lakam.

O ye mother of wisdom the embodiment of warmth and affection, kindly bestow upon us purity, nobility and consciousness so that we may become duyajas (twice born). Do endow in our possession long life, vitality, progeny, comfort, fame, security, peace and perfect stillness of mind. In thy abode do we seek refuge ye mother do grand Dow unto us the nectar of deathlessness

****

Om asatoma sadh gamaia. Tamasoma jyotir gamaia. Mrityoraama amritaam gamaia. Agyaan natam hatha kaar pragyaa prabha jagado maya mesha mitha Kar shubha staya may lagado, mrityu yantra chira kar hamko Amar banado medha sudha pilakar aatmay grahaas jaanado.

Lead us oh Lord, from unreality and falsehood, unto reality and rightiousness from darkness of ignorance unto light of wisdom and from death and misery unto emertality and eternal happiness.

****

<u>BRAHMA STOTRA</u>

Namaste sate te jagat kaara-naaya
Namaste chite sarva lokaa-shra-yaaya
Namo'dwaita tattwaaya mukti pra-
daaya Namo brahmane vyaapine
shaash-wa-taaya.

*Salutation to that beingwho creates and
supports the different worlds
Salutation to that Truth who is unequalled, and
who grant liberation.
Salutation to that Eternal supreme self who
pervades all regions.*

Twameva maataa cha pita twameva
Twameva bandhush cha sakhaa
twameva
Twameva vidyaa dravinam twameva
Twameva sarvam mama deva deva

*You alone are our Mother, Father, Brother and
Friend.
You are the source of our learning and wealth.
You are the God of all*

GAITRIE JAP

TOO NE HAME

Om bhoor bhuwah swah. Tat savitur
varenyam Bhargo devasya dheemahi.
Dhiyo yo nah Pracho-dayaat swaahaa.

Too ne hame ut-pann kiyaa, paalan
Kar rahaa hai too, Tujhse hi praan paate
ham Dukhiyo ke dukh ko hartaa too.............

Teraa mahaan tej hai, chhaayaa hu-aa
sabhee sthaan Srishti kee vastu vastu me,
too ho rahaa hai vidya-maan.......

Teraa hi dharte dyaan ham, maang-te teree
dayaa.....
Prabho hamaaree buddhi ko, aarya maarg
par chalaa....
Eeshvar hamaaree buddhi ko, shresh
maarg par chalaa......

CLOSING PRAYER

Om sarve bhavantu sukhinah, sarve anty
niraamayaa
Sarve bhadraani pashyantu maa
kashchit dukha bhaag bhavet...

Sabkaa bhala karo Bhagwan, sab par
dyaa karo Bhagwan
Sab par kripa karo bhagwan, sabkaa sab
vidhi ko kalyarn.

He eash sab sukhi ho ko-ee naho dukhari
Sab ho nirog Bhagwan dhandhanya ke
bhandhari,
Sab bhadr bhav dekhe sanmarg ke pathik
ho
Dukhiya na koee howe sristi me
pranadhari

*O lord inthee, may all be happy, may all be
free from
Misery, may all realise goodness and may
no one suffer pains*

YAJNA PRAATHNA BHAJAN

POOJNEYA PRABHU

Poojneya prabhu hamaare bhaava
ujj-wal keejiye
Chhor deve chhal kapat ko, maansik
bal deejiye

Veda kee gave richaaye, satya ko
dhaaran kare
Harsh me ho magn saare, shok
saagar se tare....

Ashwa-me-dhaa-dhik rachaaye,
yajna par-upkaar ko
Dharm maryaadaa chalaakar,
laabha de sansaar ko.....

Nitya shraddhaa bhakti se yaj-naadi
ham karte rahe
Rog peerit vishwa ke santaap sab
harte rahe.....

Bhaavanaa mit jaave man se, paap
atyaachaar kee
Kaamanaaye poorna hove, yajya se
nar-naar kee......

Laabhakaari ho havan, har
jeevadhaaree keliye
Vaayu jal sarvatra ho, shubh gandh
ko dhaaran kiye

Swaartha-bhav mite hamaaraa,
prem path vistaar ho
Idanna mamm kaa saarthak,
pratyek me vyavhaar ho....

Haath jor jhukaaye mastak,
vandanaa ham kar rahe
Naath karunaa roop karunaa,
aapkee sab par rahe.....

*(With clasped hands and bowed heads
we pay obeisance
To thee. Let thy Lordly form of
compassion prevail on us all.)*

AARTEE BHAJAN

Om jai jagdeesh hare, swaamee jai
jagdeesh hare
Bhakt jano ke sankat kshan me door
kare....

Jo dhyaave phal pave dukh vinshe
mankaa
Sukh sampati ghar aawe kasht mite
tan kaa.....

Maat pitaa tum mere sharan gahoo
kiskee
Tum bin aur na doojaa aas karoo
jiskee....

Tum pooran parmaatmaa tum
antaryaamee
Paar-brahma parmeshwar tum
sabke swaamee...

Tum karunaa ke saagar tum
paalankartaa
Deen dayaalu kripaalu kripaa karo
bhartaa.....

Tum ho ek agochar sab ke praan-
pati
Kis vidhi miloo dayaamai tum ko
mai kumtee....

Deen-bandhu dukh-hartaa tum
rakshak mere
Karunaa hast barhaa-o dwaar para
tere....

Vishai vikaar mitaa-o paap haro
devaa
Shraddhaa bhakti barhaa-o santan
kee sevaa....

SHAANTI-PAATH

Om dhyauh shaantir, antariksham shaantih
Prithivee shaantir, aapah shaantir,
Oshadhyah shaantih, vanas-patayah
shaantir,Vishwe devaah shaantir, brahma
shaantih,Sarvam shaantih, shaantir-eva
shaantih saa maa Shaantir-edhi.
Om shaantih, shaantih, shaantih

*May there be peace in the heavenly regions,
may there be peace In the atmosphere, may
peace reigh on earth. May the water
Be soothing and the medicinal herbs be
healing. May the plants Be the source of peace
to all. May all enlighten person bring peace
To us. May the Vedas spread peace
throughout. May all other objects
Give us peace and may even peace bring peace
to us and may that Peace come to us forever.
Let there be peace, peace, peace.*

This book is dedicated to our sons Nityanand Bharat (Nitin) and Chidanand Bharat (Jitin) on their special day July 21st 2013, where Our Guruji Dr. Satish Prakash performing their sanskaars (Janeo/Mundaan)

Love You Both

Your Parents
Rickey & Venita Bharat

Made in the USA
Las Vegas, NV
09 August 2021